Where Do You Want to Go?

Seed Learning

ZOO

playground

beach

aquarium

museum

art gallery

amusement park

swimming pool

Where do you want to go?

I want to go to the zoo.

Where do you want to go?

I want to go to the playground.

Where do you want to go?

I want to go to the aquarium.

Where do you want to go?

I want to go to the beach.

Where do you want to go?

I want to go to the museum.

Where do you want to go?

I want to go to the amusement park.

Let's learn about Italy.

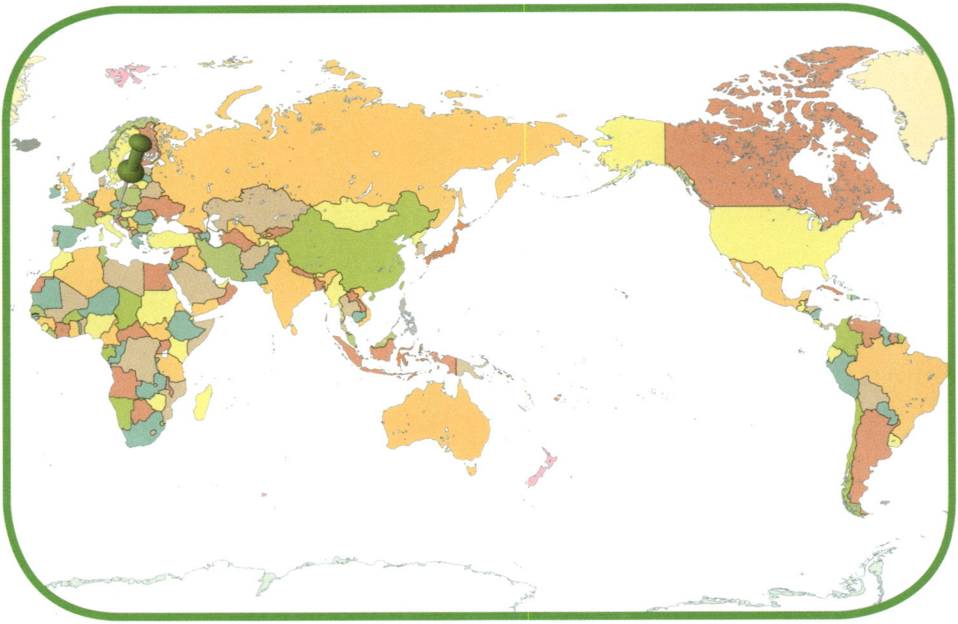

Flag of Italy

Leaning Tower
of Pisa